Taking Wing

Poems from the Oregon Outback to the Hudson Valley

Janice King

A WYATT BOOK *for* GOLDEN NOTEBOOK PRESS

WOODSTOCK, NEW YORK

Taking Wing

Poems from the Oregon Outback to the Hudson Valley

Grateful acknowledgements are given to the following publications
where some of these poems or their variants first appeared:
Catskill Poets, Outloud, Woodstock Originals, Satori,
Binnewater Tides, Poets' Gallery Press,
Woodstock Times, Ulster Literary Supplement,
Out of the Catskills and Just Beyond, A.S.K. Newsletter,
Ulster Magazine, Wildflowers, Long Shot

Published by A Wyatt Book for Golden Notebook Press
29 Tinker Street Woodstock New York 12498
Copyright © 2002 by Janice King

ISBN: 0-9675541-1-X
LC: 2002105671

Typeset by Patricia Holtz
Manufactured in Canada by WEBCOM
First Edition

For Elma DeLong King
       and
Jade King Carroll

Contents

I / The Oregon Outback

Escaped but Unfaded

In recent years I love what has been
the straw colors of summered days
our '53 pickup now junked or rusted
the ways of old men and cattle no longer here

Uncle Leonard is always on time for coffee and farm news
this forbidden machine shop is best for eavesdropping
gunny sacks sewn on jugs – then soaked
keep water cool in the fields

Escaped but unfaded
the old mare whinnies
Grandma's willow switch touches my behind
I see the heat   The wind is fierce

What matters is the song I cannot remember
memoried furrows now fallow
rest deeply in straight lines
and rhythmic swirls

The Porter Place

We lived on the Porter Place
By the time I was born,
fourteen years after the first child,
the cattle were mostly gone
Anvil and branding iron rested in the corner of the shop
By the time I was fifteen,
I remembered two droughts, a flood,
hail, two fires, a killing rust,
and one summer plague-thick with grasshoppers

But Daddy farmed and helped his neighbors
and said if someone gave him a million dollars
he'd probably just keep on farming until it was gone

Morning came up from behind Blue Mountains' rim
glowed like a rose on land with the contours of women
rolled quietly across the pasture to the Cascades' peaks,
glowed like a rose on jack rabbits and China roosters
dark red club wheat gave way in time
to a long-bearded, straw-colored strain
which wind and light weaved in a checkerboard
of fallow fields and this year's crop

Heat still rimples the air with searing waves
thick and distorted
Starlings dot fields and wires like spattered ink
Dog Star is bright and the moon turns big and orange
Harvest is over
The ranch is sold
Now what is more familiar is less real

Daddy was a farmer and a good neighbor
like his daddy and his granddaddy
and his great-granddaddy
who first plowed that land in 1875

High Plateau

On dirt of ash and fire
he took horns and danced
until his feet were hooves

Umatilla River is defined by dry banks
the boundaries of past abundance
where in August rest
moist stones and small fish bones
laid sideways in indentations
which were water

Piercing through the calm resolve of air
is the omnipresent eye
Above all else is the sun

<pre>
          blood   water
          gust   pulse
      elemental   membranes
          land   and   wing
      and air and green blade
</pre>

Hot winds
blast closed the sight
of all who bear down
on belly desert ground

Every green and crawling thing
is aware of one burning eye
Desolation is the mirage
The same terrain stretches
inside and outside a skin

The Westward Ho Room

My clothes stuck to the vinyl upholstery
when I slept in the car. I peeled awake.
At the end of Main Street is The Temple Hotel.
Kitty-cornered is The Silver Saddle
and somebody's church. Across the street
is The Rivoli Theatre. Nothing is on the marquee.

My clothes would stick to me
when I napped on the leather couch
at The Temple Hotel. Napping, waiting
for Daddy to drive me back to the ranch.
When the gift shop lady wasn't looking
I would go to the slatted saloon doors
and peek into The Westward Ho Room
where cigarette smoke and the deep fryer's
grease hazed the light with dingy motes
like a fuzzy TV or a country western Seurat.

Certain folks were always there,
in the same place, like the pool table
or the mirror in back of the bar
that Leo tended with elegant wrists
that turned at the end of each shot.
I never did see a bottle drip.
His skin was the translucent blue
of a living thing kept too long
in the dark. Delicate veins broke
across his nose and cheeks. His eyes
had no time for me or any kid.

Joy stayed hugged up in a corner booth
flashing rhinestones and tits at tall cowboys
who wore white snap shirts and never
took their Stetsons off. Bruce bellied up
to the bar, one boot on the brass rail,
well on his way to being somebody.

At the end of the bar, lit by a jukebox,
always sits a gibbous silhouette
in black lace and sequins. Josie
the hunch-backed whore
had been a seventeen-year-old beauty
when her back broke, riding with a bad boy
in a fast car. Her indigo wig made stark
the rouged funerary make-up and lipstick
shining outward in rays of ruined skin.
With a little more hooch
she knew she could still work the room.

The Pendleton Round-Up

Pungent smells of dung and sweat
bring Saturday to a dewed arena
where yesterday horses snorted
and bulls threw cowboys like ragdolls
against the fence and screams
of a beer-bellied crowd

This morning hears no Let'er Buck
sees no grandstand crowds
In back of the stock pens
and bucking shoots sits the Indian Village
Into the arena gather the Warm Springs,
Walla Walla, Nez Perce, Okanogan,
Klickitat, Klamath, Yakima, Umatilla,
Modoc, Chinook, Chehalis, Palouse,
Cayuse, Spokane sending the sun back
on dancer's silver bells and cut beads
Elk teeth, dentalium shells,
turquoise, coral and silver
shine from bodies and buckskins
The step-and-a-half dance
moves a slow circle of women
whose bright fringed shawls
sway to the drum and chant
of men who crown themselves
in eagle feathers

The Drowning of McKinley Williams

Peculiar horses grazed in the ominous
stillness of an impending storm
Under the wing of a dark sky
he jumped out of a sweat
into the river and the river
swooped him away

The beat he heard was not his blood
but the drum of the current
and a melody of fins

Going down in tight circles
his scream rushed an end
which came faster than fear

Downstream shallow waters gave McKinley back
Cold agate eyes floated up
gazing in a caryatid calmness
looking for who might find him

He is planted with doves
shaped like common rock
who sing him fossil songs
And the ground above bears
the gentle feet of a wife
whose only certainty
tastes like tears

Water and Rock

Memories lay as pebbles in streams
They had sharp edges once, but now are worn
smoothed and rounded   best suited to dreams

The salmon renews her history's spawn
These landscapes are the momentary masks
They had sharp edges once, but now are worn

Have I learned? It is difficult to ask
The currents move with or without me
These landscapes are the momentary masks

Water changes the shapes of what I see
among naked rock points and sudden cliffs
The currents move with or without me

Lapping against crawling petroglyphs
My waves find joy in breathing things that are
among naked rock points and sudden cliffs

What do I know? This seems enough so far:
Memories lay as pebbles in streams
My waves find joy in breathing things that are
smoothed and rounded   best suited to dreams

Buckskins

Morning drops its shine
on your orange skin
scented with perfumes
of alfalfa and dust

Your copper countenance
beckons the brood mare
who knows your flank
as a tongue fit salt lick

Plaited breezes shake a rattle of nettle
and play bone stalks of dry grain shafts
to the exact movement of dappled light

Aunt Annie

Aunt Annie played an accordion
      and bred Great Danes
      She sang cowboy songs
      lumberjack and beer-drinking songs
           not country western

And was married seven times
      to good men in the time when
      women tolerated them when they weren't
      but Annie never tolerated much
           fair's fair

So Annie was married seven times
      She had been Queen of the Round-Up
      could ride any horse
      liked the ones with
           spirit best

Horses knew Annie
      Knew her as the absence of spurs and quirt
      sensed her need
      to have a free head
           and run

Summer

Home is sweet atop my big bay
who would buck at a wrong blown leaf

I smell the heat through dust and dreams
"Now out of the West, Queen of the 1965 Pendleton Round-Up..."
I wave to my Blue Mountain grandstands

Here a gaucho clearing the pampas
hoeing tumbleweeds with Spook at a gallop

And then, young and strong, a Umatilla woman
moved with pheasant grace
a home on lodgepole pine at my back

I am these hills, softly rolling desolation,
will ride free in unpeopled fields
and measure time by a wheat stalk

Connect

I come to me through another
know my wariness in his eyes
can hear my laugh as he speaks it
feel what his eyebrow feels
I have in my most me
a cherished one
full of piss and vinegar
wild as a mad woman's eye
smooth as a dust devil looks
uncompromising, kind,
stubborn sonuvabitch
full of beer and too much love
who told me when I was seven
that there were more horse's asses
than there are horses
and has attended me in doubts beyond
those I let myself remember

Dark-eyed man   color of new leather
stamped with his Grandma's mark
grown on cattle and wheat
bred from demanding stock
favorite of old folk
charmer of babies
collector of masks
handy on a ship as in a barn
principled, international hometown boy
who would rather be from Helix
in all ways most undeniably with me
as solid as true ever was
I have a brother

on visiting the family burial ground

pronounce aloud the names
toward their silver ear bones

love these lacy remains
skeletons fleshed in recollection

what endures is a trophy
in the raffle of ashes

Hope

Everything as before   nothing disturbed
except my spheres and a moment or two
I am with you alternating disgust and fearful compassion
Wish I could confront you like your empty glass
and dull pain and terrible truth
without the twisted drunken mercy of unthought

Your hope is a possibility long dead and intently unlived
a protected might-have-been safe from the retribution of unequal love
This and a bunch of rolled-up prayers
in an "Inspirations" box to be read when the idea of sleep
is worse than the transgression of waking

I have stepped over winos and bottles of sweet grape tokay
past vodka and strange men's jackets
have awakened to a different brand of cigarettes
on the breakfast table than yesterday or the morning before
and have taken and given blows just to say I'm here

Had a rolled-up prayer of my own
that after the men and the pain
after the fists you absorbed with an oblique tear
after years of sitting on your words
and eating screams for supper
that after this you could recall
the defiant goodness and warm eyes
the knowing grin of resolute humor
that hope is and you are
now masked by a thin and finely applied veneer
of scars and whiskey too long worn
to remember your own solid wood
too fierce to ask for
too proud to look at hope
except in a box of tear-stained prayers

Just Before the Clearcut

Fragments of a robin egg sky
dangle in the clouds
The sun pierces lake ripples
to cast herringbone shadows
on the silt and pebbled bottom

Brown trout jump out and in
mending the surface
A bullfrog's gut-bucket twang
resonates past the singing
of its song

Deer scat mounds on moss
where hooves mark
soft and giving ground
Young huckleberries hang in milky hues
below squirrels performing high-flying

quadrilles to and from nuts and seeds
birds will never have
and they will never find
A new logging road gnaws a line
into thick beryl green clusters

of Douglas fir, pine and blue spruce
Breaking above the tree line
stand monumental gray stumps
remnants of the last bucking and falling
Old slash fire ghosts

Flowered Daggers

You have seen your demons
and met them with daggers of lilac and pine
have stroked these spirits
with the repetitious tears of moon scarred nights
then with a passion of cleansing fire
asked them in for pie and coffee

I have been held by the wall
of your hermit's cabin
to see you serve dead men wine
and cry on your mother's shoulder
then gone three years
and know your god is more with you than mine

Your bitter cud of laughter
offers congeniality to a hell
of ideals placed high above the common hope
Still, you wear the disappointment
of these impossibilities and for this I love you

I have seen you reel, dancing in pain
to your own screams of a woman howling
denial of her brother's death to a star rich sky
Wanting it so bad
I thought I heard breath returning

You did not lie or shelter eyes
to lead me feel injustice a reality merely impolite
Showed me birth of chick, lamb, pup and kitten
gave me life
Nurtured the great unloved lost
with a rage that dared defeat
and cried at the 6 o'clock news
who held me on her lap just last year

Your life is so densely loamed
that when your hour wanes
we shall stand, all of your seed,
honoring a dream to scatter you among pine needles
in the mountains, close to the clouds
where Indian Paintbrush will flame
above the earth of your ash

The Woman Cuts My Bullshit to the Bone

After weeks of writing poems and throwing them away, I called my
mother to tell her I had decided to become a jeweler. I had the good
fortune to be sitting in front of my typewriter as she delivered this
lecture. This is her poem.

Go have sex or go for a walk
Look at a blade of grass or at a formation
of clouds   Even the cracks in the sidewalk
are interesting if you look at what you see

Keep your sense of humor   Relax
and it will come to you in the dark
You are taking this life too seriously

Remember what I taught you   Stay positive
If you want something   Ask for it
The most anyone can say is   No
Never be a sheep   Never follow the crowd
for comfort's sake

and give my granddaughter a kiss

If you are in a position under authority
and being abused   Say   Yes sir   No sir
and under your breath say   And
piss on you Sir

Remember can't doesn't do anything
Remember what you have

Shake out your hands
roll your neck around
and yell Bullshit
You know you'll never be boring

Tell yourself you are just as good if not
a little bit better than anyone you know
Remember you can take just as much shit
as anyone can hand out
and always a little bit more

And   Sweetheart
if that doesn't work
you might try praying

The Odd and Certain Few

All those you really loved
Will always be alive for you. — Akhmatova

my mother loved being high on B12 and vodka

my mother loved the way light
played colored glass in a window
loved the history of common folks
and the way she could use dead trout
to make wild trees take root

she loved the soft fluttering sound
of starling flocks as they flew from wires
and clouds   as a child she popped corn on cloudy
days and laid down to try to match the shapes

my mother loved all small children and
the faces and hands of old people who knew
the smell and sight of all that flowered

my mother loved colors that didn't go together
the barn was turquoise and its roof was red
she loved sweet new potatoes
and the glinting waters
of a wind-teased lake

she loved walking the mountains
she loved nature's defiance of man
and everything sprouting and new
she loved how time and temperature split the day
and the ways she could incite the anger of petty people
she loved the odd and certain few

my mother loved her refusal to believe
in any idea that could limit
she loved the way she could see the future
and hold onto the past
she welcomed anything that got in her way
and reveled in the chaos out
of which we try to make order

she loved a righteous fight
and proving the prevailing attitudes
were most always wrong
my mother loved insisting and winning

my mother loved suffering for what she believed
she loved the rapture of pain deeply felt
my mother loved the aliveness of herself
and my mother loved me

Tollgate, Oregon

Went back to the cabin last year
up on the summit of the Blue Mountains
and looked hard for tiny olive-green tree frogs
swarms of blue-winged dragonflies
and those finger-sized black-and-yellow salamanders
even the dreaded leech
We used to have to take salt with us
when we went swimming because of them

Over by Uncle Lester's cabin used to be
this fiery patch of Indian Paintbrush
And across the lake by Jesse's first place
was a big old beaver dam

But waiting for that chorus of bullfrogs
to keep me from sleep
is what finally made my heart cave in
It is just too damn quiet
You know, most all my memories gave way
to insecticides meant for mosquitoes
and shit, I never got bit so bad

Book House
of
Stuyvesant Plaza

Locally Owned.
Truly Independent.
One of a Kind.

Knowledge

Passion

Character

Personality

Community

s e n s e™

Independent Bookstores
for Independent Minds

The
LITTLE
BOOK
HOUSE

Serving the community for over 26 years.
489-4761 *Albany, NY* **bhny.com**

Book Notes

That is How the Story Goes

I stood on the kitchen table talking
to God when I was four years old
That is how the story goes
An incident augmented in retelling
a concurrence of details over supper

My friends were old folks
I didn't understand why other
children laughed   I had been
around before   That is
how the story goes

My first trout was a fifteen-inch-long
rainbow   I was proud   The picture says
so and that is how the story goes

But what of the reliving of a moment untold
that particular taproot of a stance or
fear   a circumstance without narrative
the unending replay of perhaps?

The summer after kindergarten we stayed at the lake
There was a babysitter
and pictures I didn't understand
Eyes dripping like blackberries
with the inclemency of a command

A thudding door
a shower stall with the curtain drawn
My hand held against a hot toaster
until I promised not to tell
and the next day a fever

Beyond this is a precise amnesia
a membrane of forgetfulness
I keep my promises
I do not tell this story
Not even to myself

Hey Jesse

—for Jesse Kidwell

Down this shadow-flecked path
a transparency standing five foot nothing
greets me in gray fedora, black suspenders,
a flannel shirt and Frisco jeans over Red Wings
Your smile lost itself to me a long time ago
and your eyes faded a little
but I've always liked hands
and yours, time freckled, touch me now
in a stillness I just remembered could happen
patting soil round a just planted tree
soothing a wounded chipmunk
or dancing your knife down a whittling stick

All this magic while your eyes bolted stories
of old-timers and blizzards
of a butterfly fed on honey through winter
and Woodard's ghost skiing the frozen lake
You taught me much old man and loved me more
Since you left, when I was a kid,
I always hoped you'd be among the first I'd see
when it came time to cross over
Couldn't come back here
until a long time past when you died
of shingles   Oh Lord, I saw you once
and knew there was hardly any justice
These mountains were partial at best without your step

Standing on your home spot now
Only the outhouse is left   Funny how they endure
We dug up an aspen today for my daughter
a shoot from the trees you planted at the old HOT L
where your brogue thickened nightly to Scotch
I was your Brown Eyes
and you were my landscape   my mountains
They aren't partial now, only a little different
You and your trees are still here
I know
I saw Mom nod when we walked past your place last night
and down by the lake I heard a faint whistle
of "When You Wore a Tulip a Sweet Yellow Tulip
And I Wore a Big Red Rose"

under embedded rocks
on omnifarious clouds
in smells which place me then
on old women's calloused hands
in the perpetual resonance of memory
and in the endless variations of alphabets
I look for the little answers

on the backs of stallions
in the eyes of enduring souls
within the cadence of emotion
in the hollows of stones
in my grandmother's prayers
in dreams of dust and shifting winds
I look for the little answers

I believe
in a web of spirits
that the wise have no language
which will speak to tyrants and fools

I believe
in kissing malachite
and in blessing magpies

I believe
that the raiments of grief
are washed clean with tears
that we are the prisoners of self-imposed exiles
that we can live our love into the world

I believe
everywhere is a voice that moves

and I believe
that voice softly speaks the little answers

Amen

Oregon Eclipse

Daylight made more brilliant
by an infringing moon
holds half the sky

An awkward quiet takes the sparrow

Quivering copper ripples glow on mute starlings
who feel a silhouette of ultraviolet rays
fade into the corona violated night

A slowly returning sun sends forth apricot waves
to cheatgrass and a desert of lost instincts

With their sagebrush rhythm ravaged
cows and horses stare senseless
in the middle of the road

The stars had come out

Buckhorn Lookout

Kestrels dive toward the old stage stop at Zumwalt
No homes for twenty miles; no cars for the last twelve
just summer cow camps in the sweet wide
serviceberries blossoming, two great horned owl
chicks in a nest, buttercups, fuzzy arnica, bluebells,
white-tailed deer, red-tailed hawks
and tender spring phlox

Life the cowboy way   Cows come first
Here are pastures with paints and quarter horses,
llamas with lambs, colts and calves
right up to Buckhorn Lookout
where a serrated edging of trees
tickles an opacity of sky
Diorite and granite wear the story
Cloud shadows move light on the canyon
and the Imnaha River is a silver ribbon
unfurled across the bottom

The Snake Museum

And who except some nostalgic poet, in love with difference for its own sake, would yearn for a world where ugliness is still possible.—Leslie Fiedler

Portents at the death of Caesar,
the phoenix and the narwhal,
relics, singing fish
and the lodestone are trifles

relative to the five-legged calf,
the three-eyed kitten
and conjoined puppies
with a single tail who float in jars,
pickled at The Snake Museum in Idaho

Grandma Sara said it was a sin
to display and profit from such misfortune
Yet sin, like quicksilver,
moves resistance or no
and profit displays the piety of rutting pigs

I saw these oddities of nature
as travelers who had escaped
the cruel monotony of Procrustes' bed
Wonders to challenge a dull and exacting prettiness

Here were actualities worth preserving
matters of fact full of comfort and terror
signs not symbols of prodigies
heirs to a universe of unintended consequences

Tumbleweed

My pulse is a tumbleweed on the wind
No apparent destiny presents herself
and I impose none
When I laugh is what I love

I envy the security of focused intent
but to me
things come to me
and for now
I dance carelessly
barely remembering the ground
A tumbleweed
waiting for a gust of heart
to dance me away

II / Postcards

These poems refer to postcards painted by Franz Marc and sent to Else Lasker-Schüler in the years 1912-1914. They had met in Berlin, where they formed a lifelong friendship. In 1910 they collaborated on a poem "Reconciliation," in which he provided a woodcut and she the poem.

Lasker-Schüler performed her poetry in the persona of the warlike Prince Jussuf of Thebes. In Marc's painted postcards, he painted her fictional kingdom and elevated her to Emperor Jussuf Abigail I. In turn, she deemed him Der Blaue Reiter, The Blue Rider, high priest, court painter, and her royal half-brother.

Franz Marc died in battle at the age of 36. Else Lasker-Schüler received the Kleist Literary Prize in 1932, though the Nazis banned her work. She settled in Palestine in 1937, the year Marc's work was banned and confiscated. Works of the Jewish pair were featured in the Nazi exhibition of "Degenerate Art."

The color paintings may be viewed at The Golden Notebook's website: www.goldennotebook.com

Postcard / Little Sacred Calf

And the prophesy comes down to us
On the morning you ascend your throne
a little calf will nap in the palace grove

Birthed in a moment
when divinity touches stone
her red jasper hooves
will mark the path
of your reign and her eyes
whispering of garnets
will scatter across
the green schist of Spring

Postcard / Two Blue Horses

Fear is   mating is

Chrysocolla stallions
poised for peerless dance
twist and rear
slice the air
with glancing hooves

Fear is   mating is

on the wind
Turbid dust flies
in coral clouds

Blue fury frames
one Spring flame of cypress

A black line snakes
down each salt spine
the matrix of mane and tail

Postcard / Prince Jussuf's Lemon Horse

Colored by intrusion's scent
the bull spins and charges
Snorting
fills a canyon
with his own air
Signs claim to the edges
of rogue rye and thistles
with hoof glyphs

His horns poise to break
the possible fall
from high atop granite ridges
of a yellow appaloosa
a lemon-skinned filly
blanketed with slate spots
Her taut flank ripples
against the sky
Abstraction of morning
appaloosa sunrise

Postcard / Monkeys

Into the bursting
        branches
you reach your furred
                finger
tip a stem weighted
        with rain
plink a drink
      from a palm flower cup

Swing
      with prehensile
      sensibility
from red shadows
      to tropical
      rain   bow
         and
chase your monkey mate
       in a flash
       of flesh

Postcard / Ibex

Stone solemn
an ibex rises to meet
the charred earth
of his own red-eyed grief
No effortless gait
leads to weightless bounds
Tired legs find a cave
of sandstone walls
Suffering halts mid-stride
to surrender hide
to the mountain
This final offering
strips the hunt
from his predator

Postcards /
The Tower of Blue Horses
Yellow Seated Female Nude
Dancer from the Court of King Jussuf
The Three Panthers of King Jussuf

On a tower of blue horses
stars' lambent sheen
and moons' lunar arch articulate
a configuration of pensive muscles
There is no breeze to bear
neigh or whinny   In stillness
one senses delicate quivers
on soft muzzles
of pre-dawn stallions

Below
in a valley
a girl sprouts
desires of dark daffodils
She flowers nude
from red earth hips
Green swan grasses glide
about her

In the court of King Jussuf
is a dark woman dancer of Möbius moves
who requires no ground
on which to play her step
Harmonies flow in diaphanous folds

Three panthers are primary and celestial
each a sleek gravity with its own orbit
Their sensibilities form a den of sinews
Franz   a sapphire cat   defends nothing
Maria climbs rubicund and firm
The amber panther is Else
a poet
She hangs on black cliffs
and hisses at the moon

III / The Hudson Valley

Two Lines Straight Up

—for George Rickey

To smooth the changing drifts of air
I want to lift in argent arcs slow and wide
easing into a subtle glide

To grace away from what is rooted
on the slim embodiment of a wing
to be perceived as some unworded thing

To be burnished by the inlet light
unnoticed but by those who envy flight

Bookselling

He puts himself in the way
sighs of annoyance do not make him wince
      He leans into the Science section
      selects a hardcover and opens it in the middle
      scratches his not quite red not quite brown hair
      and smells his fingers

He is as real as the ritual
which verifies, separates, alleviates
a predicament of unobligated hours
      On Sunday he arrives at 3:00
      and waits to become the closing
            He delays after the first announcement
            after a gentle and general suggestion
            to select and purchase
            until his persistent presence prompts
            an inevitable   I would like to go home now

These mechanics only make him more vague
His clothing, his carriage, the apology of his stance
beg philosophical considerations
If he stands in the bookstore and I do not look at him
does he exist?

Four years of Sundays   every Sunday
Blizzard, hurricane warnings, freezing rain
when communication is down save for the DJ's
request that people stay in their homes
            I walk to work   He drives to town
            Occasionally there are the two of us
            for an afternoon
            I shelve and straighten
            He practices the subtleties of obstruction
            Excuse me   Pardon me   May I get past

Every damn Sunday
Today signaled by an Excuse me
He inhaled deeply
as if to create the space I required
            Look   I advance   sharpening each syllable
            I need to be exactly where you are
            Rising from behind his biblio-horizon
            he almost met my eyes
            Really? I didn't think anyone needed
            to be exactly where I am

Calligraphy

In every poem there is a painting
In every painting there is a poem—Su Shih

Mountain
Who writes the poem
You articulate above the fog
Mists make tangible an emptiness
between these epistolary strokes
of pine and your effortless
breathing calligraphy
Reflecting the rooted lines of day
nocturnal brushes shadow snow
under an ineffable moon
whose full measure
does not mean more
than to be

Becoming

Eye rivulets run to
crevices of epidermal erosion
No conservation keeps
this scape timeless
or fertile
My small and momentary
geologies
haven't the patience
for eons
Instead tectonics
shift in seasons
Vital rotations
elemental and certain
exfoliate the grace
of outward detail
by layers
to reveal a core
of mineral composition
becoming more concise
and crystalline
while weathering
time

Dream Wings

In visioned sleep
beaked with hollow bones
I leave these sad feet
     and weighted eyes
to see tree points
spread in circles
       spirit   breast
       surge to wing beats
       borne up now
I have dreamed myself whole
and am no longer human

Jade

Exact attitudes shape her body
wrap it around a sound
Legs and arms are full of larks
nesting in my eyes

She is a dark iris
gracing the air
in perpetual unfurling
Motion is fulfilled

What is written in music
is covered by skin
Lyrical sinews
sculpt the wind

The Composer
—for Baikida Carroll

He pulls birds from his bones
weeps ballads into a silver horn
and fills the darkness with long
tones and dissonance

This is not a gentle thing

He seeks unheard rhythms
and angles towards their sound
Chords incise his cinnamon skin
The notes convolute his brow

This is not a gentle thing

A song is the space between us
I have learned to sleep
within its phrases
Refrains modulate my dreams

This is not a gentle thing

As he pushes sound to chink
the silence   one cannot measure
the ways he sings

Hemphill

—for Julius

Roi Boyé
large & intentionally altered
on lamé and cognac
A rogue   raucous & refined
fresh as dimes on a flute

I recall you
a song wearing red
a dancer of the barefoot winds
blowing harmonies up
in syncopated flight
raw   &   lush
robust from Texas

Papa Blues
in his own perfect time
squawking at the sun

Rest Home

—for Stephen Barr

Motel pictures hang on green confining walls
an insipid still life and a covered bridge
Night is rendered with antiseptic smells

        Oh old friend
        speak lightly with Anna
        in the approaching dark
        They do not believe she visits then
        or that her red hair
        is spread out against the dawn

Isolation defines your shape
being fed bland food by distant hands
that never stop to touch the face they feed
The aimless advance of unmarked days
the rise and fall of shades
has set your eyes in a gaze of caged circumstance
Necessity disregards a wanting heart

        Your fierce and quirky humor
        is a resented challenge to these people
        who are the majority of your fate
        a fate of dry and colorless words

Here is your terror of life among the many
One's own hands look stranger by the hour
Tranquilized until you barely sit
They have taken away your teeth

        There

Now you cannot make fun of God

Destination

Neither of us is suited for compromise
nor for the settling of second best

Perhaps the fact I did not
let you read aloud to me

Perhaps the fact our love
was incoherent and incomplete

Perhaps it was our armoured souls
tempered by each other's rejections
and the loneliness and solitudes we grew

Perhaps the rages of disappointment
which now resign us
to each other's memory
Memory that may someday mellow
into a fondness for the past

And looking at the ocean I think
of when we slipped salt and wet
into each other
and now this floundering in regret

And the way our lovers' guttural noise
has echoed into hollow sounds of neglect

And of how our destination
has been reached
Who could have guessed
this is where we were going

Holy, Holy, Holy

I live on the edge of town
where I pray with a desiccated heart
to the Saint of Forsaken Tears
to the protectress of barren trust
I whisper novenas through dusty teeth
My tongue is undisturbed by repentance
My mouth rests quietly in retreat
churning only in the mastication of hope

Death has many feet
The charts and the cards are blank
I live on the edge of town
There are evil clowns outside my door
The woman in army blankets bays at the moon
she lives in the underworld
and deals drugs from beneath the bridges
scurrying like a troll
She was a middle-class mom
Was it a garden?   a fence?   a bed?
that grew her mad or was it the raging
parables of crack and thorazine
I live on the edge of town

The hairs on my head hurt
and my left ear is in pain
I do not need the torments of a saint
I have this obstinate vision
and a passionate array of disbelief
This is so beautiful I cannot stand it
and the pain in my left ear
means nothing

I live on the edge of town
where I give an odd man a tambourine
and accept daily blessings from a retired lawyer
who has chosen to become a mute Buddhist
I live with a girl who hates me
She is my daughter   I am delighted
by the nonsense of love whose power
it is to torment   My tears are moldy
They have staled in all of this joy
I live on the edge of town

Small Town Talk

—dedicated to The Truth and Decency League

Fictions shaped as weapons
by cunning hands and mouths
wound embarrassment with arrows
of endless chatter
and throw names like knives

Flint words spark sharp tongues
to encapsulate and dismiss another's pain
with edges so whetted they cut themselves
I am beleaguered by this hour's
acceptable morality and by the ease of lies

Did you fashion this sordid strategy
with glib intent or cynical glee or
with an arrogant responsibility? We were friends
and I am not so politic as to read these things well
You were stone and metal when we met
and your polished curves, no bones protruding,
tricked me to think your roundness would be soft

I should like to flaunt the fine neutrality of air
Still one cannot but espy how one's fiction grows
And, tell me, does the innuendo sound clever yet?

Ludins Field

Mountainous cumulonimbus float shadows on the last
chicory and Queen Anne's Lace in Ludins field
while sweet clover, timothy and ferns flow in the wind
We lease a little light from the continuum

and play our moments out between ground and sky
The flora is translating itself into fall
An initial release of yellowing leaves dots the green
Each season is singular
and each one makes folks complain

This hardy green August offers a plethora of bees
and white butterflies fluent in the surge of blossoms
Last year was brittle and dull-colored by now
the dry grasses moved with ticks and beetles

Today two red hawks hover   It is more than I asked for
Breath rises against great absences which define memory
A mourning dove insinuates his melancholy song
into the leafy glimmers of light edging the meadow

Looking at the music I notice the oddly perfect margin,
the tree line's bottom branches and the field's beginning
With night comes rainwaters foaming across bluestone
breaks in the swollen Mill Stream

Water bucks and twists white in the downpour
Its soft gurgling vowels murmur into the air
Far off a coyote hears the water's story
and sings it back to the darkened stonebird of the moon

The Barn Burner

Drunk in the dusky shadows
he consigned old barns to ashes
with his blazing flares
Delivering a monograph on fire
he initiated red sunsets
to tear apart the smoking sky
and watched flames lick timbers
to the ground with their reductive tongues

He cleared the land of the lie the barns told
There were no farms left
just expensive cars and fancy gardens
and names he did not want to know

The barn where they caught him
the one he tried to torch before
the one that still would not catch
set on what had been his family's farm

What trapped him was his inability
to extinguish his boyhood, his young manhood
Those rafters refused to fall
to the fervor he carried

I Never Soar

I never soar
but being a poet
occasionally I
move a hair's breadth
above the ground
separated imperceptibly
from the earth

The Alchemy of Stone

—a paradelle for Carol Zaloom

Aurelio said rock was turned to clay
Aurelio said rock was turned to clay
so she could perfectly fit doors into sky.
so she could perfectly fit doors into sky.
She perfectly turned clay to sky Aurelio,
Rock said, so doors could fit into was.

What old song played while the monoliths danced?
What old song played while the monoliths danced?
swaying an incalculable patience of stone
swaying an incalculable patience of stone
The monoliths swaying while what incalculable
song of patience played? An old stone danced.

On cave walls pintos gallop through millennia.
On cave walls pintos gallop through millennia.
A woman knows them. Hear their neighing?
A woman knows them. Hear their neighing?
Hear woman pintos gallop on their neighing walls.
A cave knows them through millennia.

An incalculable sky was perfectly turned.
Clay into rock monoliths swaying so the cave
doors of patience danced. A woman knows what
the song played while she fit pintos on millennia.
Their walls said to gallop through stone.
Old Aurelio could hear them neighing.

Elegant Muscles

When in unguarded ardent improvise,
Hips move with rhythms of wet intention;
Skin wants the caress of another's eyes

Offering some new intoxication.
Lips yield to mouth as kisses expand
And hips move with rhythms of wet intention.

Mingling scents entice an eloquent hand
Where push urges parting of fur soft thighs.
And lips yield to mouth as kisses expand

Into libidinous touch singing cries
While tongue's elegant muscles opens folds
Where push urges parting of fur soft thighs.

Rapid bloods reach for unceasing thresholds
On the surge and ease of generous flesh.
While tongue's elegant muscles opens folds,

Our shivering release seeks to enmesh
On the surge and ease of generous flesh.
When in unguarded ardent improvise
Skin wants the caress of another's eyes.

Ganymede

—for the painting by Arleen Cooper

A rapacious light ruts the budding
thicket that branches into young limbs
Darkling raptors flutter under skin
wing and dive with molten sight
into empurpled longings

Lift towards open swellings
voicing cries liquid as sorrow
Talons clench their prey and soar
or hover over lingering surrender

Release arrives by clutching deeper
into the spasms of liquid sorrow
until the raptor and the prey
join each other in darkling flutter

The Mythology of Flesh

The mythology of flesh wanders
bound to fragility and longing

Moss whispers to the stone what the stone never hears
Secrets told to no one lift and harden in the starlight

People fall away like ripe fruit
It is the riddle shaping our hours

Stamens pierce the night with an exactitude of hyacinth
Impulse finds its own way

Your touch is alchemy
and I am a web of fireflies

Picking Raspberries

Rows of brambles round
with sugar weighted
berries. Eyes are drenched
in dangling dark red
fruit. Elliptical
seeds are coated in
fat translucent skin.
Raspberries let go
their hold to the thought
of a touch. Once caught
the full flavor yields
to the pressure of one's
lips. Juices make tongues
a dangling dark red.

• • •

Three lifting crows et cetera the birch
My soul is no easy chair
What is true is rarely right

These events mock intention
In the attempt to reconcile
I abandon my pride and still fall

This poem is as erratic as I
Three crows et cetera the snow
before and after   Wings ink

gestures on a white sky
arcane messages scribed
in a forgotten language

And these words mean less
than if they had never met
Three crows et cetera their own departure

Lot's Wife

Escape for thy life; look not behind thee —Genesis 19:17

This grainy picture accentuates the distance
Although the present has better resolution
          it lacks character

He smiles so brightly here, slightly out of focus
Delayed sighs seep through laugh cracks
          nothing is forever

Is it a touch or a man I miss?
As with the detail
the paper in which he stands is faded

Even the fighting wasn't so bad   after
My scrapbook sweetheart punctuates
          all he left:

this sofa, that table and the space about me.
Late I find, having looked back once too often
          I taste only salt

What is Noble Love?

The flower of your breath
awakens me in the darkest part of night
Your speech lingers on
until I mistake it for my thoughts
and I have no guile
with which to polish this verse

.

Morning opens touch tempered thoughts
in sinuous sways of curve and hair
Nestling entwined warm skin
has chests sounding drum deep
from last night's stars and fire sighs
and today I feel giddy in my bones

.

The sweetest side of our tongues
quickens the blood to commit
a soft and supple sindance
to an a cappella nerve song

.

Baby with you
sunrise just keeps on
coming all day long

.

I am a woman
of varied age
within a day
I look quite young
when I've been laid

Sorrows of Water

The broken water of my mother
    binds me to a floating world
        and to dark runnels of sex
            begging forgetful currents to wash
            clean and to yield the holy nothing
                Stygian rivulets flow
                through my eyes carrying
                oaths salted with melodies
                of my supplicant sighs
            and panic sweats
            liquify the night airs
        diverting damp words
      hidden in my mouth
    half-formed syllables
of the unspoken sorrows of
water which bind me to my end

Learning to be Motherless

Along the Rondout
I walk alone
through dry leaves
speaking to Elma
Just a cold wind
and a crow
answer back

•

Hardly anyone holds the surprises
of my ornery dead mother
This strange grief misses trouble
Her flinty soul still makes a racket in my past

Tonight I would rather sort through old photographs
accompanied by an arpeggio of jiggers
than answer the phone

•

Mama, what is that you said?
Vengeance is a tailored memory
Nothing is so calculating as pity
Recollection suits the mood
Never sacrifice truth for fact

Although it has been twelve minutes after three
for nine days now, I have no sense of rest
What makes a clock decide to stop?

The Glass Merchant

The glass merchant
fears the rattle
    the wheel
    the thunder

What makes a man traffic in wares
wrapped in whispers and cotton?

What makes a man try to turn
a profit on inevitable ruin?

Perhaps he can hear the sounds
of festival bells in the breakage

The Roots Loosen

I hear dying

Dry winds chatter the brittle shake of once lush leaves
Buds dry unopened on straw stems
Bushes planted in this drought enduring soil
entwine each other in desperate wither
and fade from a climate I wonder if ever was
hoping for blooms   yearning to feel green and new

I grieve

Strains of a garden occur to me
thoughtfully tended   mulched with care
where rain anointed the breeze
and subtle shoots raced to sun and color
I believe it was only last Spring

and I cry

Roots crawl over rocks
to the memory of some small stream
The trilobite skims mid-stroke in shale
a quiet witness to the still and utter change
The flow has ceased in calamity
Cycles are abandoned in disappointed anticipation
Was it Spring?
Or did my need create the dream?
Acts of clocks and men
mock the tears of what was supposed to be
The roots loosen

and I remember

Half notes

Liquid birds
     ice-feathered
          glide by rock clouds
               flocks of bubbles fly
          in hollows of thinnest freeze
             Migrating gales
     split plumed ice
into crow tones

•

Crows in the March snow
the small one jumps
to catch flakes
A prayer comes
Let me be little
and foolish

•

Fireflies flicker the darkness
I pulse in a parcel of stars
Milk-white flames streak
across an inky sky
a night of melting light

•

Your quest is absurd and essential
the object of your love is tarnished
yet your heart is whole
The evils are real
I do not see them
Here is your weapon
I am only Sancho
You go first

The Logic of Salt

I want to feel
waves of breath
infused in being

to taste the sea
which is present
in my blood

to know necessity
to celebrate
the logic of salt

Singularities on the Coast

The bedrock cleaves
Across the fault
lies a dog skull
Albino bone roses
seem to issue from
a blade-thin fissure

An abandoned path of stone
advances toward the sand and
the impeccable conclusion of water
Constellations shift and the tide
is written in an alphabet of starfish

A conch holds what it has been told
Crustaceous lips to ear whisper
a story which in the telling
forever repeats its own absence

Umeboshi

—for the print by Carole Uehara

Blossoms   food of the immortals
appear before the leaf

Branches   bear a flowered weight
in rustic grace

Pillows   scented with you
and the evening's plumdark breeze

Umeboshi   salted to curative fullness
darkened red with shizo leaves

Nori   a bed of seaweed
where this friend to rice lies

Dreams   of tart skinned fruit
and you come to me offering

Umeboshi   the essence that lingers
is lost to inattentive tongues

Original Skin

If I could tap the bitterness of untouched thorns
which protect invitings of rose-purple furlings
where lush concentrics contain lavish
melodious moves of possible blossom

If I could harness palpitations of a heart
dwelling in longing to be wanted aches
and allay the wound of you upon my eyes
or soothe the blood between my ears

If I could heal inherent contusions
with a balm of young fingers
and appease insinuations of a past muddled
between what was and what seemed to be

If I could suture the gashes of fear
and wear their marks
in ruddled stripes
of patterned flesh

Then because scars are thicker than original skin
perhaps the agony of rose-purple petals
could open
hushing the history of my armed spine

If I could, lavish melodious moves
might form your lips across my nights
and with a balm of young fingers
soothe the blood between my ears

The Begonia's Lesson

Take the light in early
Stay moist and shaded in the heat of day
Be lush in your flowering head
Appear unrestrained and absolute
Let your delicate petals fall
as if they meant nothing

One Deep Breath

Lucid summer colors
flare from within
Vivid aspens shimmer
in the streaks of a leaf-broken sun
Emblazoned sky of lapis lazuli
stranger to clouds
whose chameleon rays
alight on scent hone hues
of stippled woods
A wild profusion
of Sweet Joe Pye Weed
chicory and yellow mallow
is enclosed by a woodpecker's
syncopation and florid cardinal
wings glinting past birches

Lake

Early morning mists
ascend to mackerel skies
in elemental mingle

Skimmers' water webs
spread silver in
a silent glissando

Tintinnabular
red maple flowers
almost sound

Turtle

She
resurrected by Spring
to swim a rippling swale
claws up a hummock
tufted with curling
cinnamon ferns

        Gauging a maximum bask
        she heaves towards the sky
        Light sun-splinters off the
        dome of her algae slick shell

With redwinged blackbirds
and grackles her blood rises
quickened by a solarium
of thawing swamps

            Twilit air
            settles to a chill
            Her splash is
            a mudward dive
            to drowse in soft
            delta earth flesh
            and a muffled chorus
            of Greek peepers

The Bones

From the clutch's elliptical egg
cracked a hatchling
an old water stone walker
venerable armoured breather
beaked she-turtle hissing
a solemn Triassic dream

Under horny ringed scales
carapace plates are knitted
through intricate millennia
joined by bone bridges
to the subtle plastron mosaic
of belly shell

Birch white bones wait
under the bluestone overhang
to claw back to an eternal wetland
bearing witness to the scope
of a hunter's eye

Gardening

Admiring the tenacity of natural growth
I pull around the strongest weeds
assert their dominance as my intent
and hope for flowers

It is best to cherish simple
and thriving things
So in planting I select flourishings
in colors and shapes a child can name
and prefer cosmos, zinnia, daisy and lily best
They are big, bright, bold and common
like me

The Cicadas Return

Roots and rocks aligned
the emergence begins
from the breathing soil up into the night
towards an ethereal epiphany
of wings   then light

More complex with each ensuing molt
cicadas perch aside their nymphal skins
The reflective arcs of garnet eyes, at last uncased,
poise unearthly in a dark and vertical world

What grants them purchase becomes a chorus tree
where males churr and thrum their estrus songs
above the purling streams

To this coded hymn of being
to the tymbal's crazed vibrato
to the shrill carousal of synchronous desire
She arrives with genital yearnings for perpetuity
What entomic muse intones this song?

When in mysterious rituals they have mated
males sing themselves to a slap-happy death
and females slit twigs to hide fat eggs
which hatch to drop into the dreamy loam
where beaks seek roots to suck the sap
of new beginnings

TAKING WING: *Poems from the Oregon Outback to the Hudson Valley* is the second joint publication of Golden Notebook Press, owned by Ellen Shapiro and Barry Samuels. The first was a book of photographs, WOODSTOCK LANDSCAPES (ISBN 0-9675541-0-1) issued with John Kleinhans's Precipice Publications. It included 57 color and black-and-white photographs by Kleinhans with an introduction by Gail Godwin. A Wyatt Book Inc. was last associated with St. Martin's Press, which published nearly one hundred titles, chiefly first fiction and narrative non-fiction.